HENRY OSSAWA TANNER

Landscape Painter and Expatriate

Celebrating BLACK ARTISTS

HENRY OSSAWA TANNER

Landscape Painter and Expatriate

Enslow Publishing
101 W. 23rd Street
Suite 240
New York, NY 10011
USA
enslow.com

CHARLOTTE ETINDE-CROMPTON AND SAMUEL WILLARD CROMPTON

Published in 2020 by Enslow Publishing, LLC.
101 W. 23rd Street, Suite 240, New York, NY 10011

Copyright © 2020 by Enslow Publishing, LLC.

All rights reserved.

No part of this book may be reproduced by any means
without the written permission of the publisher.

Library of Congress Cataloging-in-Publication Data

Names: Crompton, Samuel Willard, author. | Etinde-Crompton, Charlotte,
  author.
Title: Henry Ossawa Tanner : landscape painter and expatriate / Samuel
  Willard Crompton, Charlotte Etinde-Crompton.
Description: New York : Enslow Publishing, 2020. | Series: Celebrating black
artists | Includes bibliographical references and index. | Audience: Grades 7–12.
Identifiers: LCCN 2018016391| ISBN 9781978503625 (library bound) | ISBN
  9781978505377 (pbk.)
Subjects: LCSH: Tanner, Henry Ossawa, 1859-1937—Juvenile literature. |
Painters—United States—Biography—Juvenile literature. | African American
  painters—Biography—Juvenile literature. | Expatriate painters—France—
  Paris—Biography—Juvenile literature.
Classification: LCC ND237.T33 C76 2019 | DDC 759.13 [B] —dc23
LC record available at https://lccn.loc.gov/2018016391

Printed in China

To Our Readers: We have done our best to make sure all website addresses in
this book were active and appropriate when we went to press. However, the author
and the publisher have no control over and assume no liability for the material
available on those websites or on any websites they may link to. Any comments or
suggestions can be sent by e-mail to customerservice@enslow.com.

Photo Credits: Cover, pp. 3, 86 Hulton Archive/Archive Photos/Getty Images;
p. 6 (DSI-AAA) 14646, p. 56 (DSI-AAA) 12359, Archives of American Art,
Smithsonian Institution, Washington, D.C.; p. 11 Library of Congress Prints and
Photographs Division, Washington, D.C.; pp. 16–17 Kean Collection/Archive
Photos/Getty Images; p. 21 adoc-photos/Corbis Historical/Getty Images;
p. 24 Copyright © North Wind Picture Archives; pp. 28–29, 39, 62, 78–79 Paul
Fearn/Alamy Stock Photo; pp. 30–31 Everett Collection Historical/Alamy Stock
Photo; pp. 34–35 ND/Roger Viollet/Getty Images; pp. 42–43 Henry Ossawa
Tanner, *Daniel in the Lions' Den*, Los Angeles County Museum of Art, Public
Domain High Resolution image, www.lacma.org; pp. 46–47, 58, 68–69 Art
Collection 3/Alamy Stock Photo; pp. 50–51 Heritage Images/Hulton Fine Art
Collection/Getty Images; p. 65 Bygone Collection/Alamy Stock Photo; pp. 74–
75 Print Collector/Hulton Archive/Getty Images; pp. 82–83 Fine Art/Corbis
Historical/Getty Images.

Contents

1 A Rising Family 7

2 Making of an Artist 15

3 From the City of Brotherly Love to the City of Light 23

4 Expatriate Life 33

5 *Resurrection* and *Annunciation* 45

6 The Height of Fame 55

7 World War I 64

8 Heavy Losses 72

9 Tanner's Legacy 82

Chronology 89

Chapter Notes 92

Glossary 95

Further Reading 97

Select List of Works 99

Index 101

About the Authors 104

Sarah Miller Tanner and Bishop Benjamin Tucker Tanner raised their seven children with a strong grounding of faith and responsibility.

Chapter 1

A Rising Family

Henry O. Tanner was the firstborn of seven children, in what can only be described as a remarkable family. His father was Benjamin Tucker Tanner, a pastor in the African Methodist Episcopal Church. Eventually Benjamin Tanner would go on to become a bishop whose fame spread to all parts of the United States. Henry Tanner's mother, Sarah Elizabeth Miller, was a person of great gentleness and compassion: Tanner later declared that only her gentle touch sustained him during a childhood filled with illness and physical weakness.

Decades later, when he became the foremost African American artist, Henry Tanner signed each painting the same: Henry O. Tanner, with a heavy underline to the words (see illustration on page 86). Few people, except for close friends and family relations, knew what the "O" stood for, however. Tanner was born in Pittsburgh, Pennsylvania, on June 21, 1859, three short years after the abolitionist John Brown carried out a sensational—and controversial—attack on slaveholders in the Kansas Territory. Tanner's parents gave him the middle name Ossawa, in honor of Osawatomie, the Kansas village where the attack occurred.

HENRY OSSAWA TANNER: *Landscape Painter and Expatriate*

At the time of their son's naming, the Tanner parents had no idea that John Brown was poised to strike again. In October 1859, just four months after Henry Ossawa Tanner's birth, Brown and twenty associates attacked and nearly captured the federal arsenal at Harpers Ferry, Virginia. Had Brown succeeded, the story of the Civil War, and emancipation, might have been different. But Brown's failure and his subsequent execution as a traitor made it dangerous to invoke his name. Family members, therefore, kept the meaning of the middle initial "O" to themselves.

Family Strength

Great men do not always have great sons. The burden of competing with a famous or powerful father is often too difficult. But in the case of Benjamin Tucker Tanner and Henry O. Tanner, there is little doubt that the father's greatness acted as a spur to the son.

Born in Pittsburgh in 1835, Benjamin Tucker Tanner frequently described himself as a "Pittsburgher of three generations."[1] He was especially proud that most—perhaps not all—of his ancestors had been free African Americans for several generations. Benjamin Tucker Tanner had a powerful drive to succeed—and to glorify God in so doing. One of the few African Americans of his day to obtain a college education, Benjamin Tanner entered the ministry about the time his son was born. The bishop's notebook and diary, preserved at the Smithsonian Institution, reveal him as a person of exceptional inner strength, a man of powerful moral convictions. His wife was equally remarkable.

The Tanners were adept at keeping secrets. This is one reason why Sarah Elizabeth Miller's story is not well known. But from the writing of a great-niece, we learn that Sarah Elizabeth Miller was born in slavery in Virginia (now West Virginia) and that she and several siblings escaped via the Underground Railroad. Sarah Elizabeth's mother packed several of her children in a wagon one morning and sent them off to freedom in Pennsylvania. She, however, remained behind in slavery.[2]

Very likely, Sarah Elizabeth Miller's mother died in slavery before the end of the Civil War. By then, Sarah had married Benjamin Tanner, forming a marriage and partnership that would last a lifetime and forge a powerful legacy for their seven children.

The Civil War

Though they themselves were not enslaved, Benjamin Tanner and his growing family were very conscious of the Civil War and its importance, both to African Americans and the nation at large. They lived in Washington, DC, for a short time and even after moving to Philadelphia, the Tanners were not far from the scenes of carnage. The Tanner family's faith sustained them, however. Regardless of how many sacrifices or tragedies were involved, they saw the Civil War as a vital step in the direction of official emancipation for all African Americans.

By 1864, the Tanners lived in Philadelphia, which became their permanent home. Henry O. Tanner grew up the happy and beloved eldest child in the family. That he was loved by his parents, and that God favored the Tanner family, never seemed questioned. But this did not mean

The Underground Railroad

Though there were some African Americans, such as Benjamin Tanner, who looked back with pride on three generations of freedom, these individuals were an outstanding exception. The vast majority of African Americans in the early nineteenth century were enslaved, either condemned to live an unfree life or forced to risk their relative physical safety for the prospect of freedom. The Underground Railroad was a network of men and women who helped fugitive slaves escape, hiding them and giving them passage to free territory.

The "railroad" metaphor extended to the various roles that advocates took on— "stationmasters" would turn their businesses or homes into "depots" where slaves could hide as they made their way along secret routes toward freedom. Sometimes a "conductor" would gain access to a plantation by posing as a slave, sneaking runaway slaves north by cover of night. Many of these conductors were escaped slaves, like Harriet Tubman, who put themselves back into harm's way for the sake of freeing other men and women.

Though they lived in Washington, DC, for a brief time, Benjamin Tanner soon moved his young family into a house in his home state of Pennsylvania.

things were easy. A great-niece later recalled Benjamin Tanner's attitude toward food: "Food was never considered a matter on which one should spend precious hours of his life. I can so well remember that we children were not even allowed to discuss what we enjoyed eating. The attitude of our grandparents was that food was to be eaten only to keep the body well, so that one could work, not give pleasure."[3]

A family photograph, taken around the year 1890, confirms this notion. Benjamin and Sarah Tanner are seated in the middle, with seven children and one grandchild grouped around them. All the family members are well dressed, doubtless in their Sunday clothing, but there is a solemnity to the photograph. Assuredly, this was not a family given to frivolous behavior or the fulfillment of material desires. Henry O. Tanner stands to center-left of the photograph. Handsomely attired in a suit and striped tie, he nevertheless seems frail when compared to his father, who possesses great presence. The striped tie does suggest an artistic temperament, but viewers might conclude that here is a young man who will follow his father's ways. Perhaps he will become a minister; then again, he may use his painter's brush to illuminate biblical themes on canvas.

Powerful Parents

To be sure, one can ask whether the Tanners were actually as solid, and firm of purpose, as they appeared. Many families may have a renegade, the troublemaker, as well as the dutiful children, but this was not so for the Tanner family. Benjamin and Sarah Tanner set a powerful example. Of their seven children, one—Halle Tanner Dillon Johnson—became the first black woman to practice

Washington or Du Bois?

During the late nineteenth and early twentieth centuries, the African American community was philosophically split. Some favored the leadership of Booker T. Washington (1856-1916), who emphasized the importance of learning trade skills like farming and demonstrating hard work and forbearance in the face of racial discrimination. He believed that equality would naturally follow.

The other principal black thought leader of the time was William Edward Burghardt Du Bois (1869-1963). Du Bois did not think that equality would simply be granted by white men and women who were impressed with the virtues of black Americans. Instead, Du Bois believed it was up to exceptional, college-educated black men and women to lead the charge for equal treatment under the law.

The Tanners straddled both sides of this debate. Their working-class roots were evident, and they did not lose the common touch. At the same time, they were a good example of what Du Bois called the "Talented Tenth," the African Americans who would lead their fellows.

medicine in the state of Alabama and served as a resident physician at the Tuskegee Institute, under the leadership of Booker T. Washington. While Halle Tanner made history in the field of medicine, Benjamin and Sarah Tanner's eldest, Henry Ossawa Tanner, would go on to be a celebrated artist whose landscape paintings drew international acclaim.

Chapter **2**

Making of an Artist

Some people seem born to paint. Others seem born to sing. There are certain artists who discover their extraordinary talents at a young age, honing their creative abilities over the course of a lifetime. For Henry O. Tanner, his artistic capacity first emerged at the age of twelve.

Fairmount Park

One weekend afternoon around 1871, Henry and his father, Benjamin, were taking a stroll in Fairmont Park, Philadelphia. The park was already large, even sumptuous, but it would soon become even greater in preparation for the Centennial International Exhibition of 1876. On this particular day, however, the event that propelled Henry was simple. He and his father saw an artist hard at work. The artist had his easel up and was sketching— perhaps painting—a middle-distance hillside with a prominent elm tree.

Twelve-year-old Henry excitedly asked his father about the means and technique. Why did the artist not employ a telescope, he asked? Why did he make the task so hard on himself? But this was not the elder Tanner's area of

The Centennial International Exhibition of 1876 was the first official World's Fair in the United States, housing many art and craft exhibits and drawing more than ten million visitors.

expertise, and whatever answers he gave were less than satisfactory. The father's lack of answers could have put off the son, but they had exactly the opposite effect. "It was this simple event that, as it were, set me on fire,"[1] Tanner later wrote.

That evening, Henry asked his mother for help. She handed him fifteen cents and, with this small beginning, he purchased some type of drawing and coloring equipment. Within days, he was back at Fairmont Park, sketching and

painting the same scene. And though he cheerfully admitted that the results were not good, young Tanner had found his life's work. "From this time forward, I was all aglow with enthusiasm…that I was going to be an artist."[2]

Student with No Teacher

Henry was a talented and well-liked student. He seldom encountered difficulty in his studies, and when he did, his father's formidable reputation bolstered him. A Tanner *had*

A Centennial Celebration

The Centennial International Exhibition, or Centennial Exposition, took place in 1876, celebrating the one-hundredth anniversary of the signing of the Declaration of Independence in Philadelphia, Pennsylvania. From May 10 to November 10 of that year, the exhibition was held in Philadelphia's Fairmont Park. The exposition teemed with new inventions and technologies, featuring exhibits like Alexander Graham Bell's telephone, the Remington Typographic machine—otherwise known as a typewriter—and the right arm and torch of the Statue of Liberty, which would go on to be fully assembled in 1886.

to succeed—there was no other option. Henry graduated from high school in 1877. As valedictorian (in a class of ten) he delivered an address on the subject of compulsory education. The chances are that he had some strong feelings on the subject. His own experience would, in the course of time, prove more valuable than schooling.

The greatest difficulty lay in finding an art teacher. Philadelphia was then the jewel in America's artistic crown (that honor had not yet shifted to Manhattan), but young Henry Tanner found it virtually impossible. Tanner was a light-skinned African American; there were times in life when he could "pass" for white, even if the people who outwardly accepted him were skeptical about his background. But as he tried to find a teacher, Tanner made no attempt to disguise his ethnic composition, and he consequently had miserable experiences. One art teacher did take him on and charged him two dollars for the "lesson" of drawing straight lines.

After being turned away from one studio after another, Tanner concluded that "No man or boy to whom this country is a land of 'equal chances' can realize what heartaches this question caused me, and with what trepidation and nervousness I made the round of the studios."[3] The reason, to be sure, was racial prejudice.

Realizing he could do better on his own, Tanner abandoned the idea of studying with a master. Working on his own, he sketched and then painted a wrecked schooner off the coast of New Jersey. Tanner accomplished this during a school vacation, and the painting soon brought some attention.

Early on, Tanner resolved to become America's next maritime painter. He did not know of Winslow Homer, the artist who was achieving great things off the coast of Maine, but even had he known, Tanner would have gone right ahead. This dogged stubbornness was part of his makeup, an inheritance from his father. But Benjamin Tanner was not always in the right, and on one occasion his stubborn sense of resoluteness nearly wrecked his son's health.

Physical Challenges

Henry Tanner had a delicate constitution. Usually thin and sometimes physically weak, he plodded through life, always being aware of and respecting his limits. Coming from the Tanner family, he naturally believed that health and well-being were not one and the same—that a person could enjoy many of the good things of life even when not in good health. This type of "mind over matter" was part of the Tanner family ethic, and through sheer determination, Tanner made it to the age of seventy-seven. He was a prime example of an old expression: "the creaky gate that lasts forever."

Immediately after he graduated, Tanner was introduced to the flour business, an industry that had made many fortunes in Philadelphia. Benjamin placed his son in a flour shop, thinking the hard work might be the making of him. To the contrary, Henry became ill and nearly died. Only a series of visits to the Adirondack Mountains of northern New York State allowed him to recover his health. By the time Tanner returned to Philadelphia, the family quietly agreed that he was free to follow his artistic vision, wherever it led.

Higher Education

Tanner probably could have gone to a traditional liberal arts college. His desire was so clear and intent, however, that he only aimed in one direction: the Pennsylvania Academy of Fine Arts. The precise details of admission and how his tuition was paid are murky, but by the age of twenty-one, Tanner was a student at the academy, where he met an outstanding teacher in Thomas Eakins.

Born in Philadelphia in 1844, Eakins was only fifteen years Tanner's senior, but those years might have been twice that number in experience. A superb "nature" painter, Eakins was already well known for his realistic depiction of outdoor scenes. Sometimes the realism he depicted was too

Making of an Artist   21

A well-respected realist painter and art teacher at the Pennsylvania Academy of Fine Arts, Thomas Eakins saw potential in young Henry Tanner and became a mentor to him.

intense; some of his paintings were rejected by conservative boards and agencies. Eakins was an excellent teacher. He had no false modesty—he knew he was a superior painter compared to his students. But Eakins wanted his pupils to develop their own style, and so it was with Henry Tanner. Many years afterward, Tanner recounted the strongest and clearest teaching he had received:

> I had made a start on a study, which was not altogether bad, but very probably the best thing I had ever done. He encouraged me; but, instead of working to make it better, I became afraid I should destroy what I had done, and really did nothing the rest of the week. Well, he was disgusted. "What have you been doing? Get it, get it better, or get it worse. No middle ground of compromise."[4]

There are many artists—of that time and our own—for whom this would *not* be good advice. Very likely they would be too discouraged to proceed. But Eakins saw great potential in his student, and he prodded him so effectively that Tanner took this as one of his life mottos, applying it to his personal conduct, as well as his art.

Chapter

3

From the City of Brotherly Love to the City of Light

Tanner's father was a Pittsburgher of three generations of free black men who made his home in Philadelphia. Tanner was a Pittsburgher-turned-Philadelphian, who found it necessary to cross the Atlantic Ocean to experience personal freedom. Like his renowned father, Tanner never changed his mind. Once the move was made, the relocation was permanent.

A Business Venture

Tanner did not officially graduate from the Pennsylvania Academy of Fine Arts. But his studies were not the issue; once again, it was the ugly specter of racism that raised its head. As the only black student at the academy, it is no surprise that he would have faced prejudice and discrimination.

24   HENRY OSSAWA TANNER: Landscape Painter and Expatriate

After leaving the Pennsylvania Academy of Fine Arts, Henry Tanner set off for the South, setting up a photography studio in the growing city of Atlanta, Georgia.

The details are somewhat hazy. Tanner seldom, if ever, spoke on the matter. But from the autobiography of another artist—one who studied at the same academy—it seems that Tanner was tied to an artist's easel and left in the street one evening.[1] The manner in which he was tied resembled the crucifixion, and this may have been a not-so-subtle commentary on Tanner's religious faith.

Shortly thereafter, Tanner left the Academy of Fine Arts to begin painting on his own. He made headway, first in the painting of maritime scenes, and then in the painting of animals. He showed a special skill in the drawing of lions, which he saw at the Philadelphia Zoo. But Tanner felt pressure from his family, a need to carve a path his younger siblings could follow.

Birth Order

Psychologists and sociologists often claim that birth order is one of the most important of all factors in a person's development. Eldest children, such as Henry Tanner, tend to be self-motivated and highly disciplined, as well as unnecessarily critical, both of others and themselves. Youngest children tend to require a long seasoning, or period to develop. Of course, there are exceptions to the rule—the outstanding youngest child and the slacker eldest. But there is no doubt that Henry Tanner's single-minded approach to his art, and his cheerful manner in the face of all sorts of difficulties, closely resembles the psychological model of the eldest child.

Tanner in the South

After several years of illustrating for magazines, Tanner decided to start a photography studio. His artist's eye would be put to good use, he reasoned. The more he examined the situation, the more convinced Tanner became that Philadelphia was not the right place—there was too much competition. He, therefore, joined art with business and opened a photography studio in Atlanta, Georgia.

Tanner was not a "natural" southerner, nor did he take readily to the South. But of all the southern cities he could have chosen, Atlanta was among the best. Atlanta was a charming city in the late 1880s, however, and one of the better places for an African American, regardless of social or economic rank.

Tanner later commented that the photography studio lasted only a few months. He founded it with the intention of executing fine art in his "spare" time, but he soon found he had more time than was necessary. Few people came to his shop, and Tanner only extricated himself with the financial help of a friend of his father.

Joseph Crane Hartzell was a Methodist minister-turned-bishop. A good friend of Bishop Benjamin Tanner, Hartzell befriended Henry Tanner, rescuing him from the debts accumulated by the failed business. Hartzell then found Tanner a job teaching art at the recently founded Clark University in Atlanta. A grateful Tanner later painted Bishop Hartzell's portrait.

There is no doubt that family and friends often assisted Henry Tanner. He was a self-described "lucky" person, who often got through difficult situations unscathed. Tanner also made good use of his opportunities. In 1889, he left Atlanta during the warm summer months to spend time at the Highlands in western North Carolina. There he encountered numerous African Americans whom time had passed by: they were living a generation or two behind the times. Tanner took many photographs and made early sketches. One of these later turned into a fine painting, *The Thankful Poor*.

In *The Thankful Poor*, Tanner places an old man at the left and a young boy at painting's center—both have their hands raised in prayer. All of the action of this painting takes place in one room, and a rather run-down and shabby one. Again, the viewer sees the downtrodden aspect of African American life, but also the quiet dignity and resourcefulness that also pervaded the lives of black Americans.

A Brief Homecoming

After two years in the South, Tanner returned to Philadelphia. His parents were pleased by his return. They made a point of saying that "if worse comes to worst, you always have a home."[2] But Tanner surprised them by saying he would go to Europe. He had learned all he could from American schools and masters, he declared. It was time to see England, France, and Italy.

Tanner's parents were resigned to the situation. They had long since let go of their eldest son, in the sense that they did not try to check his enthusiasms. A party was held at the time of departure, and a photograph was taken in which Henry Tanner seems jauntier than usual. Dressed in a suit and tie, he looks like a dandy, a refined person of means who has a lot of fun but does not contribute much to the world.

28 HENRY OSSAWA TANNER: Landscape Painter and Expatriate

From the City of Brotherly Love to the City of Light   29

Tanner's time in the South informed *The Thankful Poor* (1894).

30 HENRY OSSAWA TANNER: Landscape Painter and Expatriate

Henry Tanner in his Paris art studio

From the City of Brotherly Love to the City of Light

The irony, of course, is that Tanner was not a man of means—he was just skillful, even adroit, on getting by with what he had.

Setting Sail

Tanner sailed from Philadelphia on January 4, 1891, aboard the *City of Chester*. He described his maiden voyage as a rocky one, with plenty of seasickness, and, one suspects, loneliness as well. But on landing at Liverpool, Tanner showed no hesitation. He went right aboard a railroad car, and just hours later he debarked at London.

Like many an American, before and since, Tanner was taken with the architectural beauty of London. He was especially thrilled by Saint Paul's Cathedral, whose golden dome was the highest vantage point in the city. But Tanner did not stay long. Rome was his self-described final destination, so he took ship for France, with Paris as the second of his three stops. Then something quite unexpected happened. Tanner fell madly in love with Paris.

The City of Light

Paris did exert an unusual charm, or fascination, for late-nineteenth-century American travelers. The City of Light housed more artists than any other city, in America or Europe. Then too, there was a special quality *to* the light. This is what Tanner found.

Many years later, Tanner welcomed a young African American artist to France. When that young man asked him about his theory of light, Tanner replied:

> Remember that light can be many things: light for illuminating an object or for creating a mood; for purposes of dramatization as in a theatrical production. For myself, I see light chiefly as a means of achieving a luminosity, a luminosity not consisting of various light-colors but luminosity within a limited color range, say, a blue or blue-green. There should be a glow which indeed consumes the theme or subject... It isn't simple to put into words.[3]

Paris, the City of Light, was about to provide Tanner with his best visual inspiration.

Chapter

4

Expatriate Life

Tanner never called himself an expatriate. He believed that African Americans did not have the luxury of holding that status, that they were bound to serve the cause of African American progress in America. But there is sometimes a difference between one's inner conviction and one's outer appearance, and in the five years that followed his arrival in Paris, Tanner took on the *look* of an expatriate.

The Charms of Paris

Tanner admitted that life in Paris had its drawbacks. As a Philadelphian, he was accustomed to hearty breakfasts and roaring wood-stove fires, both of which were not to be had in Paris for love or money. He described himself huddled in a doorway, devouring a small croissant and longing for the hearty fare of home. As for the heating systems, or arrangements, he found them primitive. But these material discomforts did not put him off from the sheer wonder of slowly discovering Paris. Like many an American, of his time and our own, Tanner found that the great French city does not yield all her pleasures at one time.

HENRY OSSAWA TANNER: Landscape Painter and Expatriate

Paris has long been home to artists and writers, and Henry Tanner was immediately smitten with the captivating City of Light.

The change required some adjustment. Tanner had this to say: "How strange the city of Paris was…The clatter of the wooden shoes on the stone pavement, the horns blows, the songs sung, each with its particular meaning, but to me an incomprehensible din."[1] The strangeness appealed to

Expatriate Life

Tanner's artistic nature, and the attraction was so powerful that he forgot all about Rome and made Paris his permanent home.

In just a few weeks, Tanner was settled in his tiny garret apartment and he began to study at the Académie Julian, one of Paris's best-known art schools. Tanner was not always complimentary of the Académie. He criticized the habits of its students, especially the incessant smoking of cigars. But he soon found the Académie to be vital to his efforts.

Summers in Brittany

How Tanner managed it remains mysterious, but he got by during his first twelve months with a total of $365, or one dollar per day. This included his tuition. Not only did Tanner dwell in the City of Light for the academic year, but he spent each summer in the province of Brittany.

Tanner felt an initial flush of disappointment when he found the Brittany art colonies filled with English and American artists—he had no opportunity to practice his French. But the artistic plus soon outweighed the linguistic minus, as Tanner became acquainted with dozens, even scores, of artists who were fully up to date with the latest

Art Schools

The European art school was both less formal and more prestigious than its American counterpart. If one studied at the Académie Julian, for example, he was considered a person of merit and worth, regardless of how much he drank or smoked. Parisian art schools were considered the cream of the cream, and the instructors sometimes affected a laid-back attitude, precisely because they did not have to show excellence–it was assumed.

styles and techniques. Perhaps he did not encounter Vincent van Gogh or Paul Gauguin, but almost every artist slightly lower on the chain was there for the meeting. These artistic riches and community of Brittany would be vital to the development of Tanner's technique, leading to the creation of two important works.

The Bagpipe Lesson

Executed in oil on canvas and measuring 45 by 69 inches (114 by 175 centimeters), *The Bagpipe Lesson* today hangs at the Hampton University Museum in Virginia. The bright colors and intricate symbolism are still as striking as they were to viewers of the nineteenth century.

A large tree, in full flower, frames the left-hand side of the painting. Nestled beneath its branches are a teenage boy, a middle-aged man, and a wheelbarrow. The farm implement does not seem important, but it provides balance and structure for the action, which is performed by the boy. He is blowing on a bagpipe so hard it seems his lungs will burst.

Any anxiety that the viewer has over the boy's health disappears when he examines the middle-aged man, who acts as cheerleader to the boy's efforts. Resting on the edge of the wheelbarrow, the mature man gently grins at the boy, who, he is quite certain, is making real progress at his art. If the scene were in a Scottish highland, everything would seem in proper place, but both the vegetation and information from the artist tell us that it takes place in rural Brittany, the French province adjacent to Normandy.

The energy in the boy's facial expression is difficult to match, but the viewer naturally takes in the abundant green grass that surrounds the man and boy. We do not need a caption to tell us this painting is executed in springtime, and that it depicts the energy and vitality of youth. The color of green is almost omnipresent.

If this were all, we would surely credit Henry Ossawa Tanner as a fine painter, one skillful in depicting outdoor scenes. But on further inspection, we make out more details. How could we have missed the middle-aged woman, for example? Very likely the wife of the middle-aged man or the mother of the boy, she stands just beyond the pair, forming a visual triangle. She, too, looks on with pleasure and even delight. And then—much to our surprise— we make out the little girl, perhaps seven years old, who stands on the path leading to the right background. She is beautifully camouflaged by the painting's rich colors, but now we see her, and we are not certain if she is the teenage boy's younger sister or a ghost. The artist does not tell us: he leaves that to our imagination.

Only then do we gaze to the extreme left background, and now we see a village, complete with what looks like a manor house. The artist has concealed it so well that we see it only on the third or fourth look. Finally, we step back and take it all in. Here, Henry O. Tanner gives us beauty, energy, vitality, and delight, but the specter of the little girl haunts us. Now that we know of her presence, we wonder if there was a little girl who died recently and put the village in mourning. Life and death, excitement and despair— these are part of the wheel of life, the artist informs us.

Brittany and Normandy

The French provinces of Brittany and Normandy stand side by side on the English Channel that separates Great Britain from its continental neighbors. Normandy is immediately familiar: we know it as the location of D-Day, the successful invasion of the Third Reich by the Allies in June 1944. Brittany is less known today, but at the end of the nineteenth century it was a favorite destination of visual artists. From the 1860s until the beginning of the twentieth century, the Breton art colony, also known as the Pont-Aven School, swept up artists like Paul Gaugin, Walter Osborne, and Nathaniel Hill. Talented painters left Paris, London, Dublin, and Amsterdam in search of the beautiful cool weather and the sumptuous landscape scenes that presented so many artistic opportunities.

Expatriate Life 39

Completed in 1893, *The Banjo Lesson* is considered one of Henry Tanner's finest paintings.

The Banjo Lesson

Executed in oil on canvas, and measuring 49 by 36 inches (124 by 91 cm), *The Banjo Lesson* also hangs at the Hampton University Museum. Painted one year after *The Bagpipe Lesson*, *The Banjo Lesson* became even more famous.

In the foreground of *The Banjo Lesson*, an old man and young boy, both black, form the center-left of the painting (the spatial arrangement is quite similar to *The Bagpipe Lesson*). The old man is in his late fifties, but he looks a decade older because of the endless tasks he has performed and the troubles he has seen. A weariness settles around his eyes, and though he pays attention to the boy, it is clear that his mind is only half in the present—he remembers too much of the past to shake it off.

The boy is eight or nine. He stands between the man's legs and holds a fine-looking banjo. The boy's left hand manipulates the upper strings, while his right hand is on the banjo's center. We cannot see the boy's eyes completely because he is so focused on making his music. But this music isn't his alone—it also belongs to the grandfather with whom he shares this gentle and important moment.

The beauty and precision of feeling that is so evident in *The Banjo Lesson* raises a question: How did Tanner move from being an unknown American, who had tinkered with photography, to the mid-level of artistic greatness in a matter of three years? The answer, very likely, is that he possessed enormous natural talent, which was spurred by meeting so many European greats. There is the occasional American artist who was disappointed when seeing the works of the Old World masters. Tanner was not one of them. He took the lessons imparted by historic work and built on them, producing his own master works.

While Tanner was taking care of artistic business, he let his health slip. He had never been strong constitutionally, and he contracted typhoid fever during a Parisian winter. Fortunate to recover his health, Tanner headed home to Philadelphia for the first time in several years.

A Short Season

The Tanner family was overjoyed to see Henry, and he was received with all sorts of tender requests to remain in the United States. Surely he had seen enough of Old Europe by now, friends and relatives said. But the brief visit home persuaded Tanner ever more strongly that his real home—the seat of his artistic influence—was France.

Tanner's finances were at low ebb, and he sold nearly all his extant paintings at auction. This provided him enough money to return to France, but in the process he also won friends and allies. Two wealthy Philadelphians took note of the auction, and one of these—Robert C. Ogden—arranged for the purchase of *The Banjo Lesson*. Later, Ogden would go on to donate the painting, Tanner's single most famous work, to the Hampton University Museum in Virginia.

Sailing back to France, Tanner felt more inspired than ever. He had succeeded at a type of genre painting—the depiction of old men and young boys in the development of musical talent. Now he wanted to broaden his horizons. Soon after returning to Paris, Tanner went to work on *Daniel in the Lions' Den*.

42 HENRY OSSAWA TANNER: Landscape Painter and Expatriate

Expatriate Life 43

Tanner's religious background began to assert itself in paintings like *Daniel in the Lions' Den* (1895).

The Prophet and the Lions

By the year 1895, Tanner had largely abandoned genre painting in favor of depicting biblical scenes. He never laid out his reasoning, not in explicit terms. It seems likely, however, that he was influenced by two factors. His father yearned for Tanner to become a minister—and while he was not interested in the life of a pastor, he now had the capacity to deliver "sermons" with his oils and brush. The second factor was strictly economic. Whether in France or the United States, people were more willing to buy religious paintings than depictions of everyday life.

Executed in 1895, *Daniel in the Lions' Den* was shown at the Paris Salon in 1896. The reaction was mixed. A solid majority of viewers applauded the work, especially the physical depth Tanner achieved in his depiction of the prison. Though a minority, the critics made valid points. Tanner did not achieve enough with Daniel's face, they declared, and it was not clear whether the lions were truly predators or were simply there as window dressing.

To us, with the hindsight of more than a century, it is apparent that *Daniel* was a first-rate painting. Most striking is the "depth" of the prison cell in which the prophet spends his time. Then, too, the use of pale moonlight, coming through openings at the top, helps create a sense of wonder.

Tanner, as usual, paid little attention to the critics. He was thrilled that *Daniel* received an honorable mention in the Salon and continued to attract positive attention. But his first genuine masterpiece—and his first major patronage—was yet to come.

Chapter 5

Resurrection and Annunciation

Henry O. Tanner achieved a new, staggering height with *The Resurrection of Lazarus*. First exhibited in 1896, it was soon purchased by the French government.

Measuring 38 by 48 inches (96.5 by 122 cm), *Lazarus* is executed in oil on canvas. The viewer has a privileged position, deep within the cave that contains the tomb. Darkness pervades the edges, but the center of the painting is illuminated by unseen floor lamps or candles.

The viewer sees about fourteen people—male and female—at the entrance to the cave. All of their faces express wonder. The viewer's eye is drawn to the center-right, where Jesus stands, slightly apart from the others. Jesus's eyes are cast down, showing his intense concentration; his hands are slowly lifting up, as he miraculously raises Lazarus from his tomb.

A female figure, quite likely the Virgin Mary, kneels; she gives an admiring, almost worshipful gaze back toward Jesus. A bearded middle-aged man helps Lazarus out of the tomb. The resurrection is complete.

46　HENRY OSSAWA TANNER: Landscape Painter and Expatriate

Resurrection and Annunciation 47

The artistry of *The Resurrection of Lazarus* (1896) earned Henry Tanner great acclaim and a new patron.

Many artists had attempted this theme, and some, quite notably Rembrandt, had come close to success. Tanner's painting succeeds more than any other, however, and this is because he captures the precise moment when faith overrides disbelief.

In the middle of this extraordinary event, there is another significant figure. Among the fourteen faces, there is one black man. His head wrapped in a turban, the man looks as if he might be from Morocco, but his lean, spiritual features might suggest Tanner's own.

Tanner took on an enormous challenge, and he pulled it off. Though there were some critics, perhaps three-quarters of all viewers were either daunted, thrilled, or moved. It was a rare person who looked on with calm equanimity.

A Trip to the Holy Land

Heir to a large Philadelphia fortune, Rodman Wanamaker lived in Paris much of the year. He knew Tanner from both places, and he was profoundly impressed by *Lazarus*. He believed Tanner had accomplished something truly great, but there was more to do. He commented that there was "Orientalism" in the painting, but that it was by accident.[1] Wanamaker offered to pay Tanner's travel expenses to the Holy Land, saying America lacked skillful painters of Orientalist aesthetics. For his part, Tanner was thrilled.

Tanner had always been very conscious of the need to economize. This was even more important, considering he was not paying the bill. Tanner, therefore, made careful records and receipts of every expense, and the record shows that he lived at a bare subsistence level during the trip.

Tanner sailed first to Egypt and then traveled overland to Palestine. He was thrilled to see sites from the Bible and equally to interview and sketch men and women who resembled biblical figures.

In the fifth week of his voyage, Tanner returned to Europe. While in Venice, he received a telegram from a friend, saying that the French government had purchased *The Resurrection of Lazarus*. Tanner was not the first American to be accorded this honor, but there was no denying his overwhelming joy. Tanner hastened to Paris, where he was congratulated by all his friends and associates.

While the French embraced Tanner, the American press was more conflicted in its assessment of Tanner, due in part to Tanner's own reticence. A reporter for the *Boston Herald* declared that he had previously seen *Lazarus*,

Shifting Names

Today we call territory in the Middle East by proper national names—Israel, Syria, Jordan, and Lebanon. In Tanner's time, however, the entire area was still governed by the Turkish leaders of the Ottoman Empire. Because of the way Christians were treated under Ottoman rule—with fewer freedoms and more restrictions than their Muslim counterparts—Christian Europeans preferred not to dignify the Ottoman Empire with that title. They, therefore, referred to the entire region as the Holy Land.

50 HENRY OSSAWA TANNER: Landscape Painter and Expatriate

The Annunciation

Resurrection and Annunciation

and it had a powerful impact. But the artist himself was something of a disappointment: "Mr. Tanner cannot be interviewed, because he has nothing to say; that is, nothing about himself. He has no skill at grasping incidents in his life. He cannot be convinced that the reading public cares a rap about him."[2] This was highly unusual. Most artists did all they could to drum up new business and promote themselves.

Race was another inescapable issue for Tanner. The *Boston Herald* correspondent went on: "How much proportion of colored blood is in Mr. Tanner's veins I am ignorant for he has one of the faces that shows few of the familiar traits. His skin is as fair as the average descendant of the Latin race, and it is only a second scrutiny that hints of his African descent."[3] American newspapers continued, year after year, to comment on Tanner's ethnic background, while French journals did not.

The Annunciation

In 1898, Tanner embarked on his most ambitious painting to date. Each previous work of art represented a forward step, but taking on *The Annunciation*—the meeting between the Virgin Mary and the angel Gabriel—required a huge leap of faith.

Tanner had his own studio by now, and he could hire assistants when he wanted—but he still did most of the work alone. He labored over *The Annunciation* for months and finally unveiled it to the Parisian public in 1899.

Measuring 57 by 72 inches (145 by 183 cm), *The Annunciation* is executed in oil on canvas. This was one of the largest canvases Tanner ever used, and it allowed plenty

Resurrection and Annunciation   53

of scope for his ambition. The Virgin Mary sits on the edge of a narrow bed, which is framed by a red and purple partition. Mary looks like a sixteen-year-old girl, with knowledge and understanding beyond her tender age. Her face is turned up at an angle as she contemplates the arrival of the angel Gabriel. He comes not dressed in clothing or even in human form. Rather, the angel is shown as a broad but also tall column of golden light, which shimmers at the extreme left of the painting.

The viewer's eyes go first to Mary to examine her adolescent face, and then to the light source. Only later do they take in the material details. A thick Persian rug covers most of the floor; the part of the floor that is visible reveals intricate stone work. One senses poverty in the scene, but it is the type that scorns material comfort, or the things of this world. Tanner gives no caption to the work, but the viewer senses that his message is plain: *God alone is enough.*

Tanner's Faith

In the first decade of his Parisian residence, Tanner attended church regularly. But by his late forties, he gave up on most formal religion. Virtually everyone who really knew Tanner described him as a man of great faith, but it was one of equally great reserve and quietness. He remained Bishop Benjamin Tanner's son, while shaping his own spiritual journey.

The Summit

As the nineteenth century ended, Henry O. Tanner stood atop a part of the artistic world. Firmly established in Paris, but also enjoying his summers in Brittany, Tanner was the most successful African American artist to be found on either side of the great ocean. Artistically, he had few critics. But in terms of his focus, he still came under fire for not doing more for the African American community.

Tanner did contribute quite a lot to African American artists, but on his own terms. He became a mentor to younger black artists, and he supported the National Association for the Advancement of Colored People (NAACP) shortly after it was formed. On one thing Tanner was adamant, however—he would choose his painting subjects, and he would not be swayed by popular opinion.

Chapter 6

The Height of Fame

The end of the nineteenth century was an auspicious time in Henry Tanner's life. He married, started a family, and continued to turn out first-rate art. Fame did not change Tanner. His drive to create was essentially internal, and it did not vary with how others reacted to his art. Had he attained this level of fame in his twenties, the case might have been different, but he was forty-one when the century ended. His personality had long since been forged in the fire of his remarkable family—and the difficulties he overcame.

An Intriguing Couple

Fifteen years younger than Tanner, Jessie Olssen was the daughter of a Swedish American businessman. She grew up in San Francisco, but after college graduation she toured Europe. She and her younger sister both had potential careers as opera singers, but Jessie's interest waned when she met Tanner in 1898.

They made an intriguing couple. Tanner's quiet reserve lifted in Olssen's presence. Though they came from rather different backgrounds, they were united in their appreciation of art and music. If there was an obstacle to

56 HENRY OSSAWA TANNER: Landscape Painter and Expatriate

Jessie Olssen Tanner poses with son Jesse Ossawa Tanner for Henry Tanner's *Christ and His Mother Studying the Scriptures*, around 1908.

their happy union, it was of an old and familiar type: Jessie Olssen was white and Henry Tanner was black. To the couple, the racial difference never affected their feelings for one another or altered their wish to be together. They did wish to please their parents, however, and there may have been some initial opposition. But each family member that encountered the loving couple soon withdrew his or her objections. It was plain that these two belonged together.

Tanner and Olssen were married in London in 1899. Their happiness was soon complete, with the birth of a son they named Jesse.

A Welcome Reunion

Tanner was largely self-taught, but his two years at the Pennsylvania Academy of Fine Arts had certainly assisted

Interracial Marriages

In the United States, interracial marriages were rare, owing in large part to the severe discrimination faced by black Americans and deep-rooted prejudices about intimate relationships between black and white people. But even in the more progressive and permissive expatriate communities of London and Paris, there were still few marriages between black and white individuals. In America, many states, in fact, specifically forbade interracial marriages. These state laws were struck down by the US Supreme Court decision *Loving v. Virginia*, handed down in 1967.

HENRY OSSAWA TANNER: Landscape Painter and Expatriate

Roughly twenty years after Henry Tanner left the Pennyslvania Academy of Fine Arts, his teacher Thomas Eakins painted a portrait of him, seen above.

The Height of Fame **59**

in honing his technique. Then, too, Thomas Eakins stood out as a much respected and helpful teacher during Tanner's time in school. He always remembered Eakins's words: "Get it, get it better, or get it worse. No middle ground of compromise."[1]

It was a great honor, therefore, to be painted by his former teacher. Sometime in 1900, Thomas Eakins completed an impressive painting of Tanner. A seated Tanner gazes obliquely toward the viewer. The background is a dark brown, which matches the color of Tanner's suit— only his face and his red tie give the painting splashes of color. Tanner's hair is beginning to recede, but he has more than the typical man of forty. His spectacles give him a quizzical look, but there is also introspection, and no small amount of melancholy. Here is a man who knows sorrow, and, one suspects, its meaning. The painting now hangs in the Hyde Collection of Glens Falls, New York.

A Wealth of Support

As Tanner's career soared, he seldom wanted for patrons. Thanks to his father, he had a ready-made community of helpers within the African Methodist Episcopal Church community. Many were unable to assist financially, but those who could tended to be quite generous. Thanks to his own sterling efforts and the superior art he created, Tanner also received assistance from rich men. These were usually industrialists or the heirs to industrialist fortunes. Rodman Wanamaker sent Tanner on not one but two trips to the Holy Land. Robert C. Ogden purchased several Tanner paintings and donated most of them to prominent museums. But the longest lasting of all Tanner's patrons was Atherton Curtis.

A wealthy man who made his fortune in medicinal patents, Curtis divided his time between New York State and Paris. He first met Tanner in 1897, just when the artist was in the full flush of success thanks to the success of *Daniel* and *Lazarus*. Curtis was such an admirer that he and his young wife invited the Tanners to move to America, to live in a house built for them in Mount Kisco, New York.

The Tanners did make a trip to New York, but they found Mount Kisco less congenial than expected. Years of living in France accustomed Tanner and his wife to a more temperate climate, and they were appalled when the temperature dipped to -28 degrees (-33 degrees Celsius) on a January day during their visit. Once they returned to Paris from this visit, there were no more discussions of moving to America.

Nonetheless, Curtis was very helpful to Tanner. Perhaps it was through his intervention that the *Ladies' Home Journal* became aware of Tanner and made an offer for the biggest commission of Henry Ossawa Tanner's career.

Ladies of the Bible

Tanner often divided his artistic career in two sections, declaring that his early paintings mostly featured males and masculine tasks, while his later ones usually had a predominance of females and feminine pursuits. He had already embarked on this change when he entered into discussions with the editors of the *Ladies' Home Journal*.

Many new magazines had been established during the 1890s. Of all of them, the *Ladies' Home Journal* had the largest number of subscribers, averaging 800,000 per month. Tanner was pleased to be contacted, and he and the *Journal* editors drew up an agreement, under which he would furnish six "Ladies of the Bible" portraits.

The costs of this project were greater than anticipated. The *Ladies' Home Journal* eventually brought out four, rather than six, of Tanner's paintings. Critics reacted negatively to the paintings, and, for once, the modern viewer is inclined to agree. The "Ladies of the Bible" appear stiff, solemn, and inaccessible: one cannot imagine having a conversation with them. But even if the "Ladies" were less than successful as fine art, they introduced Tanner to a larger audience in the United States, where he would succeed to a greater degree with individual portraits.

Biblical Scenes

Tanner had already made his name as a painter of biblical scenes. By the year 1904, he concentrated almost exclusively on biblical paintings, and he depicted almost exclusively women.

Return of the Holy Women is one of Tanner's most successful paintings from this period. The disciple John— one of the few men to appear in a Tanner by this stage— walks slowly on the extreme right, guiding and assisting the Virgin Mary and Mary Magdalene on their walk from Calvary, where Christ has just been crucified. Sorrow and loss are everywhere evident, but something in Mary Magdalene's expression gives one pause. Is it possible she suspects Jesus will soon arise from his tomb?

Tanner also executed *The Visitation (Mary Visiting Elizabeth)* and *Christ and His Mother Studying the Scriptures.*

62 HENRY OSSAWA TANNER: Landscape Painter and Expatriate

The completed *Christ and His Mother Studying the Scriptures* (1910)

The rich oils give the biblical women greater depth and more realism than was typical of the time. In fact, by the year 1900, Tanner had surged past all rivals in the field of biblical painting—he was now the master.

Personal happiness had a great deal to do with Tanner's success. Happily married, he was now the father of a son—Jesse Tanner—upon whom he doted. Photographs from this time show Tanner the happiest he had ever been. There were more care lines in his face than perhaps he would have liked, but these reflected the price he had paid, for artistic freedom and personal happiness.

Chapter **7**

World War I

The onset of World War I caught Henry Tanner and his family by surprise. This was not unusual—they were among millions of families that could say the same. But while they may have been caught unawares by the global conflict, it was about to hit home quite literally: the Tanners' summer home at Trepied was close to the German invasion route of France.

The Invasion of 1914

War was declared in the first week of August 1914. Very few Frenchmen or Americans living in France anticipated the size and speed of the German invasion. German military planners had long expected war, and they planned for a brilliant, rapid conquest of France, to be followed by a slower conquest of Czarist Russia.

Henry, Jessie, and Jesse Tanner were at Trepied when the fighting began. They left almost immediately for England, to enroll Jesse at the Folkestone School in Kent. That completed, the parents returned to France, where they—and their neighbors—were appalled by the terrible conflict and consequent human suffering. Tanner wrote to his dear friend, Atherton Curtis, on that subject.

World War I

Though he was too old for active combat in World War I, Tanner worked with the American Red Cross in the war effort.

"One reads the papers all day," Tanner declared, "but only once in a while, thank God, does one realize the suffering and despair that is contained—a sentence like 40 killed, 400 killed, 4000 missing, 40,000 losses. How many loving, carefully raised sons in that number, how many lonely wives, mothers, children, sweethearts."[1] For the first two years of the war, Tanner was so depressed that he could not paint.

Curtis was alarmed enough to write Tanner at length, assuring him of his good works and of the virtue of taking a rest when possible. "You cannot hope to attain all that you have wished to attain," Curtis wrote. "No one does or can. You have painted faithfully and you have done some good work. You have produced some beautiful pictures, some very beautiful ones. You have also produced some that have been failures, complete or partial. Some of your pictures I have not liked at all."[2] Curtis was clearly more than a friend. He was a moral compass for Tanner, especially at times of crisis.

America Enters the War

In April 1917, the US Congress declared war on imperial Germany. The United States now was one of the Allied Powers, allowing Tanner to take a more active role in the war effort.

Tanner was fifty-eight, far too old for military service with either France or America. But the American Red Cross was active in the First World War, and Tanner believed he could contribute. He approached the American ambassador to England, who wrote a letter on his behalf to the ambassador to France.

Tanner developed a plan: to use the land around military hospitals to raise fresh vegetables. Soldiers recovering from their wounds could participate in the effort. Perhaps Tanner was not the first person—American or French—to have this idea, but he certainly was ahead of his time. The ideas he propounded later became used as therapy for convalescent soldiers.

Once the American ambassador to France was introduced to Tanner, he expressed support. Tanner was attached to the American Red Cross, with the rank of lieutenant. For the first and only time in his life, Tanner wore a uniform. A photo from 1918 shows his lean, angular features. Though he was not the typical American "doughboy," Tanner certainly gave his all to the war effort.

But as was so often true in his life, Tanner experienced a jarring reminder of the ugliness of racism. At a dinner party at Neufchateau, Tanner was in the company of several white officers, none of whom seemed directly to realize he was African American. This had long been a theme of Tanner's life because of his light-skinned complexion. One of the officers commented on how well African American soldiers had fought in the final battles of the war (the 369th US Regiment, known as the Harlem Hellfighters, being a prime example). But the conversation did not end with this compliment.

"It had been a rather gay dinner," Tanner wrote, "when Captain R_____ continuing his accounts of a trip to the front which had fired us all said 'but we will have to kill several of those n——s down home before we will be able to get them back in their place.'"[3] This appalling statement strikes us powerfully today, but it was by no means unusual

68 HENRY OSSAWA TANNER: Landscape Painter and Expatriate

Many artists had painted the famous Arc de Triomphe, but *The Arch* (1919) made the great Parisian landmark more accessible to thousands of American viewers.

World War I 69

among white American officers and soldiers of the First World War. Many of them feared African Americans would be more difficult to "manage," now that they had seen something of the larger world.

Tanner kept quiet at the dinner party. Very likely, the offending captain did not even realize he was African American. But when this captain, who hailed from Mississippi, had to suddenly depart, Tanner and others leaned forward over the table to allow him passing room.

"When he arrived at me he put his big hand upon my head in the position of a blessing—somehow I felt I had God's blessing as far as mortal erring man could give it. He was I know as blind as when Isaac blessed Esau."[4]

Was this Tanner's moment? Should he have said something at the dinner party? Many of us who read these words would be inclined to think so. But Tanner was in a delicate position. African Americans were just beginning to gain their footing in the US military. And it is hard to see what good Tanner could have achieved at that specific moment as well as that moment in our cultural history.

A Juncture in History

Though Tanner did not realize it, he stood at a juncture in the racial and ethnic history of the United States. Black soldiers *had* fought with exceptional courage and skill during the war. Another black artist—Horace Pippin of Goshen, New York—served with the Harlem Hellfighters and sketched several wartime scenes. But the heroism African Americans showed under fire seemed to win them more, rather than less, anger and suspicion back home.

Red Cross Paintings

On the very day the Armistice was signed and World War I officially ended—November 11, 1918—Tanner asked for permission to paint while serving with the Red Cross. Permission was granted, but it was made abundantly clear that Tanner should paint nothing of combat—that he could only depict Red Cross scenes.

The paintings that Tanner painted are not generally considered to be his best work. The charcoal sketches of Red Cross canteens seem forced, and the viewer does not know what message is being sent. But there were two outstanding successes from this part of Tanner's career. The first is *House of Joan of Arc (Domremy)*, which shows the sloping two-story home of the French heroine. It is an evening scene, and two American infantrymen approach the house, perhaps while on guard duty. Two other figures linger in the dimly lit doorway, and one wonders if the spirit of Joan of Arc has been invoked for protection.

The second success is *The Arch*. Executed in oil on canvas in 1919, *The Arch* is an evening scene of the Arc de Triomphe, in the heart of Paris. Built to commemorate nineteenth-century Napoleonic victories, the Arc de Triomphe became a sign of France resurrecting itself from the ashes of the First World War. Tanner captured the arch in the last moments of twilight, a scene familiar to millions of Parisians, but an eye-opener for other viewers.

Though Tanner was able to produce these paintings for the Red Cross and though his family had survived the war, their lives would change forever.

Chapter 8

Heavy Losses

The Tanners wanted life to return to normal, to the way it was before the horrors of World War I. This never happened. The great irony is that Henry Tanner's artistic fame hit its peak, at almost precisely the time that his family fortunes waned.

The Tanners were not alone—far from it. America lost 110,000 to battle death and disease during World War I, but France lost more than *ten times* that number. It was a very rare French family that had not lost someone in the war. Given that the Tanners had bound themselves to France inextricably, it is not surprising that they felt the pain of the national losses. In the two years that followed World War I, Tanner was virtually unable to paint. He was exhausted from his efforts—physical and moral.

The Tanner family also experienced dislocation and sadness in their beloved summer home at Trepied. The artist colony never recovered from the war, and the Tanners felt much more isolated than in previous times. Even so, they would very likely have been all right if not for a series of losses—on both sides of the Atlantic Ocean.

Bishop Benjamin Tucker Tanner died in January 1923. He had enjoyed a remarkable life, filled with personal and familial triumph. But his death left a huge void for other family members. He had always been the steady—if also irascible—center of the family. The Tanner branch in France felt the loss keenly.

A Trip to New York

In almost the same month that Benjamin Tanner died, Henry Tanner was named a chevalier of the Legion of Honor. This was the highest award the nation could bestow, and Tanner consistently declared it to be the highest honor of his entire life. That, naturally, raised the question of when the United States would catch up with France and do equal justice to its expatriate artist.

Tanner had already planned a major exhibit in New York City. Shortly before Christmas of 1923, he sailed. His telegrams home suggest his loneliness: "Sunday morning when we got on the boat I saw a big commotion on the dock and went to see what was up. I found them distributing letters and telegrams and unexpectedly received one too, from my dear Jessies."[1]

Arriving at New York City, Tanner rented rooms in Brooklyn and spent the next three months shepherding the most ambitious of all his showings to date. Sometime during that winter, an up-and-coming young African American journalist interviewed Tanner.

Jessie Fauset freely admitted her nervousness. Born and raised in New Jersey, she was about to become a major voice for the new generation of African Americans, but Henry Tanner was already its artistic sensation. Raised on

74 HENRY OSSAWA TANNER: Landscape Painter and Expatriate

Heavy Losses

World War I had devastating effects on France, in terms of both physical destruction and number of lives lost.

The Family Goes On

The reigning patriarch of the Tanners, Bishop Benjamin Tanner was the most outspoken and forceful family member. After he passed on, his idealism and dedication continued in the family legacy. Carter G. Woodson, editor of the *Negro History Bulletin*, printed an extensive family story in 1947, pointing out that the Tanners had supplied the world with doctors, nurses, and ministers, as well as one truly sensational artist.

stories of black Americans who had done extraordinary things, Fauset interviewed Tanner, and found—much as the *Boston Herald* reporter had—that Tanner did not think, or act, from a sense of self-promotion or aggrandizement. He had only three passions: his wife, his beloved son, and his art, in that order.

The more Fauset probed, the more Tanner deflected. He was nothing special, he declared, just a person possessed of an artistic vision. Describing Tanner as "tall and slender with grizzled hair," Fauset named him "the least affected and the least conscious of personal glory"[2] of all persons she had interviewed. Eventually, Fauset came to the question all African American journalists wished to pose: Would Tanner ever permanently resettle in America?

The answer was simple: no. Not "for all his faith"[3] could Tanner imagine coming back home to live. He noted many good things about life in America, but he declared the hustle and bustle was far too much for his taste. Thirty-odd years in Paris and Trepied had made him very content with his position on the other side of the Atlantic. Fauset was too well mannered to pose the other great question: what would, or could, Tanner do for his fellow African Americans? But he anticipated her, saying he noticed his fellow blacks were making great progress as a people. And there the conversation ended.

Painting Through Pain

Tanner returned to France to find his wife in poor health. The World War had taken a terrible toll on her nerves, and she never fully recovered. Beyond that, however, she was soon diagnosed with a severe case of pleurisy.

Tanner became a full-time caretaker, a role to which he was exceptionally well suited. He remembered all too well that his mother's tender care meant the difference between life and death when he was ill. He set up the household in such a manner that Jessie was relieved of all cares and concerns. But all his best efforts were not enough: Jessie Olssen Tanner died in France in 1925. Her husband was never again the same.

Tanner remained close with his wife's sister and her husband (both of her parents were now deceased). His friendship with Atherton Curtis remained as strong as ever. Henry Tanner interested himself in his son, whose career as a mining engineer seemed ready to take off. But in the aftermath of his mother's death, Jesse Tanner also became ill. He did not become an invalid, but his father

Destruction of Sodom and Gomorrah (1929) veered away from Henry Tanner's typically realist style.

had to keep close watch on him, and the promising career was aborted.

There was nothing left to do but paint. The last ten years of his life were not extraordinarily productive, but some of

the results were excellent. *Destruction of Sodom and Gomorrah*, executed in 1929, is one of the greatest of all Tanner's color schemes. Rather than opting for gray or black to render the smoke rising from Sodom and Gomorrah, Tanner instead suffuses the background with a rich riot of blue-green. Unlike the realism of his earlier works, the palette of *Sodom*

80 HENRY OSSAWA TANNER: Landscape Painter and Expatriate

Changing Trends

Both critics and connoisseurs regarded Tanner with something close to awe. His spectacular achievement was, to be sure, evident to anyone who examined his career. But Tanner also benefitted in a curious way from a change in the international art scene. When he arrived in Paris, in 1891, Europe was very much in the lead. By the time of his death, in 1937, America had seized that position. Tanner was, therefore, remembered as one of the last and greatest of painters of religious scenes.

and Gomorrah lends a more abstract, Impressionist feel than Tanner had heretofore employed.

Tanner's last blaze of artistic glory came in the early 1930s, when both sides of the Atlantic were mired in the Great Depression. Art sales had often been difficult throughout Tanner's life, but it was difficult to experience this—the worst of financial and economic times—in his seventies. Perhaps this is why Tanner returned to the biblical themes he painted earlier in his career.

Tanner also returned to the theme that stayed with him the longest. He had always been intrigued by the story of the good shepherd, and he had created several paintings depicting shepherds in their fields. Toward the end of his life, Tanner painted such a scene one more time, with *The Good Shepherd (Atlas Mountains, Morocco)*. The shepherd is very small in this painting. He guides his flock along the spiny edge of an enormous chasm. Tanner employs late afternoon sunlight to show the importance of morality in one's decisions. The chasm is wide and dangerous, but the good shepherd *will* bring his flock through. It is clear that even though Bishop Benjamin Tanner had passed on, his faith endured in his son.

Tanner's Legacy

Tanner's last years were spent in a mixture of work and sorrow. He continued to paint, but his heart was not fully engaged. This is hardly surprising. Tanner had always been a person for whom family and faith came first, and when he lost his wife, his entire life went steadily downhill. To be sure, there were more honors and awards. But they meant less, on almost every occasion.

Last Moments

Tanner died peacefully at home, in Paris, on March 25, 1937. He was seventy-eight years old.

Condolences came from across America and Europe. At the time of his death, Tanner was the most famous African

Tanner's Legacy

American artist, and one of the most famous America had ever sent overseas.

Tanner's son, Jesse Tanner, remained overseas for the rest of his life, dividing his time between Paris and a vacation home in the south of France. Jesse Tanner died in 1987.

And for a long time, Henry Tanner was forgotten. Of course, he was mentioned in academic textbooks and

Henry Tanner received renewed recognition when *Sand Dunes at Sunset, Atlantic City* (1885) was displayed in the White House during Barack Obama's administration.

the occasional art exhibit, but for mainstream culture, his career remained in obscurity for decades.

A Cultural Reconsideration

The 1970s were a good time for Tanner, in retrospect. Various exhibits featured his work, and a new generation of African Americans gained an appreciation for his work. He was highlighted in books and journal articles. One of the most poignant was *Henry Ossawa Tanner: American Artist.* The author, Marcia M. Mathews, asked Jesse Tanner to write the introduction, and it's deeply moving to read his account of his father's work:

> My father always worked very hard on his pictures and they were painted very slowly. If you study them you keep discovering new things about them—a new form is revealed, a new star seems to shine, a new shadow stretches out— in a word, his pictures are very much alive. A Tanner can do more than give you enjoyment, it can come to your rescue, it can reaffirm your confidence in man and his destiny, it can help you to surmount your difficulties or console you in your distress.[1]

Jesse Tanner revealed in words what many viewers had long suspected: that his father was a quiet mystic whose art flowed from his faith. Jesse Tanner went on to reveal that his father did not believe in praying for specific things or assistance from above—rather, he prayed with these simple words: "Let God guide us."[2]

Of course, while cultural appreciation for Henry Tanner's work began to grow, some of the old, familiar criticisms resurfaced: Tanner gave too much attention to European and Christian themes; he ignored his African American roots; and he should have done more to spread the effect of African American art. During a long lifetime, Tanner never responded to these criticisms, studiously ignoring them to continue making the art that was important to him. To Tanner, it was self-evident that an artist chooses his own subject and does the best he can.

Though the criticisms leveled at Tanner are fair, there are important facts to consider. As to his focus on Christian themes, Tanner was a minister's son. And Tanner's father was not just any minister, but a larger-than-life figure of such committed piety that he rose to the level of bishop within the church. It was likely natural that Henry Tanner, raised in a deeply religious household, would emphasize Christian themes to the exclusion of all others. It is also true that Tanner did nothing showy in favor of his fellow African Americans. But he rarely did anything personally showy at all, even to raise his own profile. We can return to the *Boston Herald*'s account in 1897: "Mr. Tanner cannot be interviewed, because he has nothing to say; that is, nothing about himself. He has no skill at grasping incidents in his life. He cannot be convinced that the reading public cares a rap about him."[3]

Truer words about Tanner have seldom been spoken. Tanner never cared for fame. He remained a workman's artist throughout life—one more interested in what was done than concerning the person who did it. Instead, his work was always intended to speak for itself, both to his own talent and as a demonstration of what black artists could accomplish. While Tanner did nothing to advance

HENRY OSSAWA TANNER: Landscape Painter and Expatriate

Though he never actively pursued fame or acclaim, Henry Ossawa Tanner gave all of himself to his work.

the cause of African American art other than what he accomplished with his brush and oils, the same is true in regard to Impressionism and Modernism. Tanner never saw himself as a "movement" artist, either creatively or politically: he was always an individual, intent on raising the level of his own work.

But while his apolitical stance might still be viewed as problematic, there is no denying that Tanner performed the task he assigned himself. He executed more biblical scenes than any American artist—black or white—of the early twentieth century, and he was the finest African American painter of his generation. The bishop's son used all of his God-given talent, leaving nothing to waste.

Chronology

1835
Benjamin Tucker Tanner is born in Pittsburgh.

1840
Sarah Elizabeth Miller is born in slavery in what is now West Virginia.

1856
Benjamin Tucker Tanner joins the African Methodist Episcopal Church.

1858
Benjamin Tucker Tanner and Sarah Elizabeth Miller marry in Pittsburgh.

1859
Henry Ossawa Tanner is born.

1861
The Tanners move temporarily to Washington, DC.

1865
The Tanners move permanently to Philadelphia.

c. 1871
Henry Tanner becomes interested in art while in Philadelphia's Fairmont Park.

1876
Tanner graduates high school.

1876-1878
Tanner tries several occupations; resolves on art as his career.

c. 1880
Tanner studies at the Pennsylvania Academy of Fine Arts.

90 HENRY OSSAWA TANNER: Landscape Painter and Expatriate

1889
Tanner moves to Atlanta, Georgia, to work as photographer.

1890
Tanner returns to Philadelphia.

1891
He sails for Europe and settles in Paris.

1893
Tanner returns to the United States; *The Banjo Lesson* and *The Bagpipe Lesson* are exhibited.

1895
Tanner executes *Daniel in the Lions' Den*.

1897
Tanner travels to the Holy Land; *Lazarus* is purchased by French government.

1898
Tanner travels to Holy Land for second time; Tanner becomes friends with Atherton Curtis.

1899
Tanner marries Jessie Olssen in London.

1900
Tanner's portrait is painted by his teacher, Thomas Eakins.

1902-1903
Tanner paintings are shown in *Ladies' Home Journal*.

1903
Son Jesse Tanner is born in New York City.

1909
Two autobiographical essays are published in *The World's Work*.

Chronology 91

1914

Tanner's mother dies; World War I begins; Jessie Tanner goes to England for high school; the Tanner couple return to Paris.

1917

United States enters World War I; Tanner becomes a lieutenant serving with the American Red Cross.

1918

Tanner executes several Red Cross/war paintings.

1923

Tanner is made a Chevalier of the Legion of Honor (French); Bishop Tanner dies in Philadelphia.

1923-1924

Tanner returns to New York City for extended visit.

1925

Jessie Olssen Tanner dies in France

1929

Tanner executes *Destruction of Sodom and Gomorrah*; Great Depression begins.

1937

Henry Tanner dies in Paris.

1996

White House purchases *Sand Dunes at Sunset, Atlantic City*, the first painting by an African American to be so honored.

Chapter Notes

Chapter 1
A Rising Family

1. Henry O. Tanner, "The Story of an Artist's Life," *The World's Work* (June 1909): 11662.
2. Dewey F. Mosby et al., *Henry Ossawa Tanner* (Philadelphia, PA: Philadelphia Museum of Art, 1993), p. 24.
3. Mosby, p. 27.

Chapter 2
Making of an Artist

1. Henry O. Tanner, "The Story of an Artist's Life," *The World's Work* (June 1909): 11662.
2. Tanner, p. 11663.
3. Ibid.
4. Tanner, p. 11665.

Chapter 3
From the City of Brotherly Love to the City of Light

1. Joseph Pennell, *The Adventures of an Illustrator: Mostly in Following His Authors in America and Europe* (Boston, MA: Little, Brown and Company, 1925), p. 54.
2. Henry O. Tanner, "The Story of an Artist's Life," *The World's Work* (June 1909), p. 11663.
3. Hale Woodruff, "My Meeting with Henry O. Tanner," *The Crisis* (January 1970), p. 11.

Chapter 4
Expatriate Life

1. Naurice Frank Woods Jr., *Henry Ossawa Tanner: Art, Faith, Race, and Legacy* (New York, NY: Routledge, 2017), p. 54.

Chapter Notes   93

Chapter 5
Resurrection and *Annunciation*

1. Marcia M. Mathews, *Henry Ossawa Tanner: American Artist* (Chicago, IL: University of Chicago Press, 1969), p. 80.
2. Mathews, p. 88.
3. Ibid.

Chapter 6
The Height of Fame

1. Naurice Frank Woods Jr., *Henry Ossawa Tanner: Art, Faith, Race, and Legacy* (New York, NY: Routledge, 2018), p. 30.

Chapter 7
World War I

1. Marcia M. Mathews, *Henry Ossawa Tanner: American Artist* (Chicago, IL: University of Chicago Press, 1969), p. 156.
2. Naurice Frank Woods Jr., *Henry Ossawa Tanner: Art, Faith, Race, and Legacy* (New York, NY: Routledge, 2018), p. 205.
3. Mathews, pp. 176-177.
4. Ibid.

Chapter 8
Heavy Losses

1. Marcia M. Mathews, *Henry Ossawa Tanner: American Artist* (Chicago, IL: University of Chicago Press, 1969), p. 183.
2. Jessie Fauset, "Henry Ossawa Tanner," *The Crisis* (April 1924).
3. Ibid.

94 HENRY OSSAWA TANNER: Landscape Painter and Expatriate

Chapter 9
Tanner's Legacy

1. Marcia M. Mathews, *Henry Ossawa Tanner: American Artist* (Chicago, IL: University of Chicago Press, 1969), p. xii-xiii.
2. Mathews, p. xiv.
3. Mathews, p. 88.

Glossary

abstract Not having a concrete shape or form.

adroit Highly skilled or resourceful.

aesthetics Principles that guide the appreciation of art.

apolitical The quality of not engaging with politics.

assert To make known or to claim.

auspicious Remarkable or significant; worth noting.

debark To exit a mode of transportation, mostly referring to ships, trains, or planes.

equanimity The state of being equal.

expatriate Someone who leaves their homeland to settle in a different country.

extant Still existing.

garret A very small living space.

hasten To move quickly.

impressionism An artistic style that emphasizes the representation of feelings about a subject rather than a strictly accurate visual representation of that subject.

oblique Not straight on, indirect.

Orientalism Term used for art involving elements of Middle Eastern, South Asian, and East Asian cultures.

patron Person who funds an artist's work.

progressive Supporting or advocating ideas that encourage social reform, usually in favor of marginalized groups.

quizzical Puzzled or curious.

Realism A nineteenth-century art movement that encouraged the representation of scenes and situations that depicted contemporary men and women doing ordinary things.

reticence Reluctance to speak.

smitten To like or admire greatly.

Further Reading

BOOKS

Bearden, Romare, and Harry Henderson. *A History of African-American Artists from 1792 to the Present.* New York, NY: Pantheon Books, 1993.

Marley, Anna O. *Henry Ossawa Tanner: Modern Spirit.* Berkeley, CA: University of California Press, 2012.

Mathews, Marcia M. *Henry Ossawa Tanner: American Artist.* Chicago, IL: University of Chicago Press, 1964.

Woods Jr., Naurice Frank. *Henry Ossawa Tanner: Art, Faith, Race, and Legacy.* New York, NY: Routledge, 2018.

WEBSITES

Conversation: Henry Ossawa Tanner – PBS NewsHour
https://www.youtube.com/watch?v=mxXn0hscGdA
A video discussion of Henry Tanner's life and work.

Henry Ossawa Tanner, The Banjo Lesson – Smarthistory
https://smarthistory.org/tanner-banjo
A recontextualization of Tanner's art as a black artist, focusing on *The Banjo Lesson*.

Henry Ossawa Tanner – The National Gallery of Art
https://www.nga.gov/collection/artist-info.1919.html
A brief biography of Henry Tanner.

Select List of Works

The Annunciation (1898). Philadelphia Museum of Art, W.P. Wilstach Collection, Philadelphia, PA.

The Banjo Lesson (1893), Hampton University Museum, Hampton, VA.

Daniel in the Lions' Den (1895), Los Angeles County Museum of Art, Los Angeles, CA.

Destruction of Sodom and Gomorrah (1929), High Museum of Art, Atlanta, GA.

The Good Shepherd (1903). Jane Voorhees Zimmerli Art Museum, Rutgers University, New Brunswick, NJ.

The Resurrection of Lazarus (1896). Musée d'Orsay, Paris, France.

Index

A

Académie Julian, 35, 36
Annunciation, The, 52–53
Arch, The, 71

B

Bagpipe Lesson, The, 36–38
Banjo Lesson, The, 40–41
birth order, about, 25
Brittany, France, 35–36, 38, 54
Brown, John, 7–8

C

Centennial International
    Exhibition, 15, 18
*Christ and His Mother Studying the
    Scriptures*, 61
Civil War, 9
Curtis, Atherton, 60, 64–66,
    77

D

Daniel in the Lions' Den, 41, 44,
    60
*Destruction of Sodom and
    Gomorrah*, 79–80
Du Bois, W.E.B., 13

E

Eakins, Thomas, 20–22, 59

F

Fauset, Jessie, 73–76

G

*Good Shepherd, The (Atlas
    Mountains, Morocco)*, 80–81

H

Hartzell, Joseph Crane, 26
Holy Land, the, 48–49
House of John of Arc (Domremy),
    70

I

interracial marriage, 57

J

Johnson, Halle Tanner Dillon
    (sister), 12–14

L

Ladies' Home Journal, 60–61
"Ladies of the Bible," 61

N

Normandy, France, 38

O

Ogden, Robert C., 41, 59–60

101

P

Paris, 32, 33–35
Pennsylvania Academy of
Fine Arts, 20, 23–25, 57–59

R

Red Cross
Tanner's enlistment in,
66–70
Tanner's paintings for,
70–71
Resurrection of Lazarus, The,
45–48, 49, 60
Return of the Holy Women, 61

T

Tanner, Benjamin Tucker
(father), 15–16, 19, 20, 23,
26, 27
death of, 73, 76, 81
marriage and family, 7–14
as minister, 8, 44, 53, 59,
85
Tanner, Henry Ossawa
American press's view of,
49–52, 73–76
art education, 20, 23–25,
35, 57–59
childhood and family,
7–14, 15–17, 25
criticism of, 52, 54, 84–85

cultural appreciation of,
84–87
death of, 82–83
experiences racism, 18–19,
23–25, 52, 67–69
fame, 7, 14, 44, 45, 54, 55,
59–60, 72, 82–83
health of, 19–20, 41
lieutenant in Red Cross,
66–70
marriage and son, 55–57,
60, 63, 76, 77–78, 82
moves to Atlanta, 26–27
moves to Paris, France, 32,
33–36, 41
religion and, 25, 44, 48–49,
53, 61–63, 81, 84, 85
start as an artist, 15–22
trips to Holy Land, 48–49,
59
trip to Europe, 27, 31–32
Tanner, Jesse (son), 57, 63, 64,
76, 77–78, 83, 84
Tanner, Jessie Olssen (wife),
55–57, 60, 64, 72, 76
death of, 77, 82
marriage and son, 57, 63
Tanner, Sarah Miller (mother),
8, 16, 27
born into slavery, 9
marriage and family, 7–14
Thankful Poor, The, 27

U

Underground Railroad, 9, 10

V

Visitation, The (Mary Visiting Elizabeth), 61

W

Wanamaker, Rodman, 48, 59
Washington, Book T., 13, 14
World War I, 64–71, 72
    black soldiers in, 67–69, 70

Charlotte
Etinde-Crompton

Samuel
Willard Crompton

About the Authors

Charlotte Etinde-Crompton was born and raised in Zaire and came to Massachusetts at the age of twenty. Her artistic sensibility stems from her early exposure to the many talented artists of her family and tribe, which included master wood-carvers. Her interest in African American art has been an abiding passion since her arrival in the United States.

Samuel Willard Crompton is a tenth-generation New Englander who now lives in metropolitan Atlanta. For twenty-eight years, he was a professor of history at Holyoke Community College. His early interest in the arts came from his wood-carver father and his oil-painter mother. Crompton is the author and editor of many books, including a number of nonfiction young adult titles with Enslow Publishing. This is his first collaboration with his wife.